A Quiet and Peaceable Life

by John L. Ruth

a People's Place Booklet

Good Books

Acknowledgments

Pages 4–5, material from *The Simone Weil Reader,* edited by George Panichas, copyright © 1977 by George Panichas, reprinted by permission of David McKay, Inc. Page 47, material from *I Wish I Could Give My Son a Wild Raccoon,* by Eliot Wigginton, copyright © 1976 by Reading Is Fundamental, reprinted by permission of Doubleday & Co. and the National Audubon Society Expedition Institute. Page 53, material from *The Mennonite Encyclopedia,* edited by Cornelius Krahn, copyright © 1955 by Mennonite Publishing House, used by permission of the publisher. Page 65, material from *Living More With Less,* by Doris Janzen Longacre, copyright © 1980 by Herald Press, reprinted by permission of the publisher. Page 84, quotation from *The Humility of God,* by John Macquarrie, copyright © 1978 by John Macquarrie, Student Christian Movement Press and Westminster Press, used by permission of the publisher.

Photograph Credits

Cover Credits: Fred A. Curylo (C.P.S. Photo Productions, Kitchener, Ont. Canada), front; Kenneth Pellman, back.

Richard Reinhold: 13, 33, 35, 39, 44, 46, 59, 60, 68 (bottom), 72, 81, 86, 91 (bottom); *Toledo Blade* (Tom O'Reilly): 7, 71; Dr. Schafmeister: 8; Burton Buller: 11; David Hunsberger: 14; Stephen Scott, 16, 91; Stephen Scott collection: 31; Frances Woodruff: 19; Jeff Sprang: 21; Lorena Buch: 22; Beth Oberholtzer: 25, 89; Peter Michael: 26, 63; *Louisville Courier-Journal* (Barbara Montgomery): 29; Paul Jacobs: 36; Harry Gibbel: 40, 43; Fred J. Wilson: 48–49, 75; George Reimer: 51; Merle Good: 52; Kenneth Pellman: 55; John Ruth: 56; Melvin Liechty: 64, 76, 85; *Toronto Globe and Mail:* 67; Mennonite Central Committee: 68 (top); Gary Emeigh: 78; *Des Moines Register* (Carl Voss): 82; James Hertel: 92.

A QUIET AND PEACEABLE LIFE

Copyright ©1979, 1985 by Good Books, Intercourse, PA 17534
International Standard Book Number: 0-934672-25-3
Library of Congress Catalog Card Number: 85-70284

Originally published, 1979
Revised edition, 1985

Contents

Preface

If the "Plain People" of North America are to be understood in terms of their own concerns, we must consider sympathetically their own expressions, and the biblical cadences they echo. Having maintained, with the tolerance of their society, a simple life as "the quiet in the land," these folk still prize such passe virtues as modesty, humility, and obedience to God's will, as interpreted by a disciplined community of faith. Their values, difficult to appreciate in a world bemused by progress, are seldom if ever articulated, except as curiosities, in our "mass media."

A comment by Simone Weil in her thoughtful book, *The Need for Roots,* is suggestive. "The essential fact about the Christian virtues," she reflected, "what lends them a special savour of their own, is humility, the freely accepted movement toward the bottom." But as she watched Western civilization behaving as though it had lost its center, Weil concluded regretfully that in modern culture the paradox of "a humility of a really high order is something unknown to us. We cannot even conceive such a thing possible. In order to merely conceive it, we should have to make a special effort of the imagination."

John L. Ruth
Harleysville, Pennsylvania
July 29, 1985

A Biblical Theme

From the Delaware River to beyond the Great Plains and from Ontario to Texas exist many rural communities of North America's "plain people." Ever since their 18th-century arrival on this continent they have experienced a partial victory over the logic of technological advance and secularity. Although they have been explained from time to time by historians, sociologists and psychologists (Rheinold Niebuhr called the Mennonite farm a "Protestant surrogate for the Catholic monastery"), they maintain a life and values that defy simplistic analysis.

There are well over a hundred thousand of these souls, and although some of their communities are dying or shifting into more modern and thus less visible form, many more are thriving, expanding, and spawning daughter communities in other regions. When these people move, it is almost always in search of less populated land.

The most visible are the Amish and the strictest of their spiritual cousins, the Mennonites of Swiss/ South German background. But the observer must be cautioned immediately against oversimplifying. There are equally distinct, if smaller, "Old Order" wings of groups such as the Church of the Brethren and the Brethren in Christ, both dating back to the 18th century. There also conservative "Old Colony" Mennonites with a history in Russia, and some 30,000 Hutterites, a communalist wing of the

same group that produced the Mennonites.

None of these groups is a carbon copy of another. In fact, while they often settle close to each other, they worship separately, and any superficial observation lumping them together, they vigorously refute.

Yet they do have plainness, simplicity, non-resistance, mutuality and visible identity as ideals in common. They recognize these ideals in each other, and in speaking to persons in one of the other groups, the "plain" person will readily use the phrase, "our kind of people."

Born in an era of disappointment with the state religions that once held power throughout Europe, these groups have held closely from their very beginnings to the words of Scripture. There they find the story of a dispossessed people with the dream of dwelling in a land of promise — each family under its own vine and fig tree. Their hero is less the scheming Jacob than his peaceable father Isaac, who, rather than striving with jealous neighbors over an inheritance he had laboriously restored, "removed from hence," and dug new wells.

In family Bible-reading and in sermons which usually draw extensively on scriptural passages, they hear that "God setteth the solitary in families," and are constantly reminded that "though the Lord be high, yet hath he respect unto the lowly." The kind of sacrifice God desires, Hebrew writers understood long ago, is "a broken and contrite spirit."

In the words of Mary the mother of Jesus, they hear God being thanked that he has "put down the mighty from their seats, and exalted them of low degree." They understand the Apostle Paul's admonition that they "study to be quiet," and they believe with him that among the signs of God's spirit in human personality are peace, patience, gentleness, meekness and temperance. They believe that Jesus was teaching them to see into reality when he said that "the meek" are blessed, and that, as his own teachers had taught, it is the meek who shall, in the providence of God, inherit the earth.

It is deeply ingrained in the plain people's conscience to be respectful of "all that are in authority," insofar as that authority is in principle "ordained by God." Even though they may feel that a moral craziness pervades much of the nation in the midst of whom they live, and even if they feel the government oppresses them, they pray continually for that government, and for the salvation of its officials, always with the hope, in Paul's words, that they may continue to be allowed to lead "a quiet and peaceable life in all godliness and honesty."

They are seldom equipped to venture into the marketplace of ideas with their convictions. But where their verbal statement has been undeveloped, their startling visual profile continues to raise spiritual questions in the minds of reflective viewers who are not simply tourists, but questers.

Better it is to be of an humble spirit with the lowly, than to divide the spoil with the proud.

Proverbs 16:19

Better is little with the fear of the Lord than great treasure and trouble therewith.

Proverbs 15:16

. . .The kingdom of heaven is like unto leaven, which a woman took, and hid in three measures of meal, till the whole was leavened.

Matthew 13:33

. . .The kingdom of heaven is like to a grain of mustard seed, which a man took, and sowed in his field:

Which indeed is the least of all seeds: but when it is grown, it is the greatest among herbs, and becometh a tree, so that the birds of the air come and lodge in the branches thereof.

Matthew 13:31, 32

I owe the Lord a morning song
Of gratitude and praise,
For the kind mercy He has shown
In length'ning out my days.

He kept me safe another night;
I see another day;
Now may His Spirit, as the light,
Direct me in His way.

Keep me from danger and from sin:
Help me Thy will to do,
So that my heart be pure within;
And I Thy goodness know.

Keep me till Thou wilt call me hence,
Where never night can be,
And save me, Lord, for Jesus' sake,
He shed His blood for me.

*—"I Owe the Lord a Morning Song,"
a well-known hymn written one
Sunday morning around 1890 by
Mennonite minister Amos Herr when
he was prevented from going to
meeting by snowy weather.*

My soul shall make her boast in the Lord: the humble shall hear thereof, and be glad.

Psalm 34:2

Behold, thy King cometh unto thee: he is just, and having salvation; lowly, and riding upon an ass.

Zechariah 9:9

I am meek, and lowly of heart.

— Jesus

Who among you is wise or clever? Let his right conduct give practical proof of it, with the modesty that comes of wisdom.

James 3:13, New English Bible

. . . Keep thy soul diligently, lest thou forget the things which thine eyes have seen, and lest they depart from thy heart all the days of thy life: but teach them thy sons, and thy sons' sons. . . .

Deuteronomy 4:9

Do not be conceited or think too highly of yourself; but think your way to a sober estimate based on the measure of faith that God has dealt to . . . you . . .

Let love for our brotherhood breed warmth of mutual affection. Give pride of place to one another in esteem.

Do not be haughty, but go about with humble folk.

Never pay back evil for evil. Let your aims be such as all men count honorable. If possible, so far as it lies with you, live at peace with all men.

Do not let evil conquer you, but use good to defeat evil.

—from Romans 12, New English Bible

"Not That Outward Adorning"

"Style" and "fashion" are negative words to the plain people. And, for the Amish, the term "obsolete" has little or no use. "Fashion" has to do with the wish to be noticed, or to be considered in step with the world's current taste. Both such motivations are dysfunctional in plain society.

Very early in their history, Anabaptists could sometimes be identified by their clothing — to their mortal danger. Their garb was simple and, in the course of decades, came to be old-fashioned. Refined Dutch Mennonites were struck by the clumsy, hobnailed shoes of their Swiss fellow believers. The Amish — the strictest wing of the Swiss after 1693 —insisted that buttons represented style and military clothing, as did "bearded upper lips," or mustaches. Whereas the wealthy plain Quakers of Philadelphia had plain-cut but expensively textured garments, and had pretty much given up the plain or "straight-collared" coat by the Civil War, thousands of Mennonites, Amish and Brethren still make it an issue to dress simply and uniformly in the closing decades of the 20th century.

The Swiss in general take longer than other people to make cultural changes. Rural communities from which Swiss Mennonites emerged tended to take a dim view, even before the "Reformation," of the cultural influence and legislation by which urban centers like Bern and Zurich imposed their character on surrounding regions. Bernese

"Old Evangelical Baptists" of the 1660s wrote songs criticizing the expensive wastefulness of "unnecessary" clothing. And their descendents in Pennsylvania in 1726, the Mennonites of Conestoga (later Lancaster County), had a reputation for plain dress that could attract a German mystic looking for the simple life.

Most people resent legalism, but the plain people see more to fear from the opposite extreme, a careless conforming to the present fashion. In the name of nonconformity to the world, they practice a uniformity of dress in conformity to their own community. A great many subtle variations, invisible to the naked eye of an uninformed observer, speak volumes to the plain people themselves. The color or shape of a buggy, whether or not there is a little window in the back, and whether or not it has carpet; the shape and material of the woman's cap, the color of its strings or width of its ribbons, its size, and where it is worn or perched — all these are as decisive as the streaks defining a species of bird. Clothes are a form of communication.

An Amish woman, in speaking of another Amish group slightly less strict than hers, commented, "They iron too much."

Jewelry is forbidden as unquestionably unnecessary, and functioning only as an expression of pride in one's person. Even a wristwatch becomes a problem, since it involves the question of what kind of band to have. A gold-plated cross is particularly unthinkable; to make this symbol a tasteful feature of one's personal grooming seems to mock the very idea of Christ's ugly rejection by worldly society.

One of the more striking visual phenomena in this category is the "Black-Bumper" automobile. A group of Old Order Mennonites, at the point of belatedly permitting its members to drive cars, decided to require the painting out of the chrome parts. This functions not only to restrain members' pride over shiny ornamentation, but also to establish the sub-type of Mennonite at a distance of 100 yards or more. The variations of strictness in this regard are sometimes entertaining to outsiders, who note that significant bits of chrome on the sometimes expensive cars are often excluded from the anti-pride requirement.

Another irony is that sometimes the plain coat is so similar to a clerical collar (a most un-Mennonite conception) that strangers may address an un-ordained farmer as "Father" or "Reverend."

One more example: in central Pennsylvania the various Amish groups have buggies of varying colors, representing degrees of conservatism. Surprisingly, the order from liberal to conservative is from black to yellow to white. White is the most conservative, since it comes from an earlier requirement of having undyed cloth.

. . . Let it not be that outward adorning of plaiting the hair, and of wearing of gold, or of putting on of apparel;

But let it be the hidden man of the heart, in that which is not corruptible, even the ornament of a meek and quiet spirit, which is in the sight of God of great price.

1 Peter 3:3-4

. . .Consider the lilies. . .Solomon in all his glory was not arrayed like one of these.

—Jesus

". . .Not until about 1860, or after the Civil War, did our American churches catch the spirit of pride in attire. This was brought on through numerous inventions, and from then on it grew apace. Factory-made dress materials, machinery and many other new things completely changed the American way of life. Our fathers' church leaders had a strong desire to hold on to the old way of life, and although much has changed over the years, they have been successful in 'holding the line' to the point that we have been separated from the world, which has in time created a culture different from that of the world."

—*a Pennsylvania Amish minister*

27

"Oh, these theologians! How one contrives to live inwardly in a higher world and outwardly in a lower, without damaging one's inward sincerity and without treason to the inner Kingdom of God, we are not told. This distinction between inward and outward life — a distinction of which the Gospel knows nothing — has done Christianity much harm."

—G. J. Heering,
The Fall of Christianity

Suit the action to the word, the word to the action; with this special observance, that you o'erstep not the modesty of nature.

—Hamlet, III, iii, 20

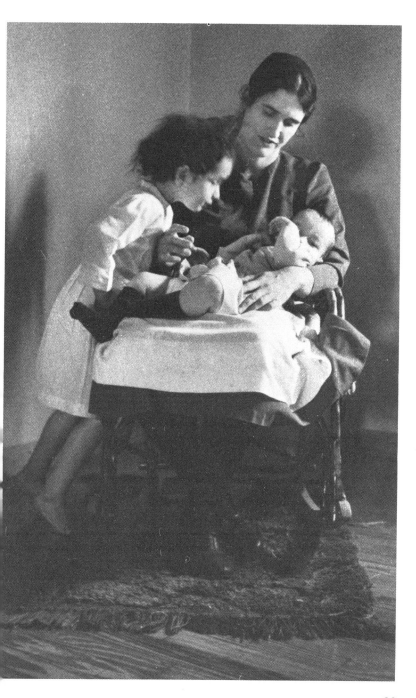

It is possible to become proud of one's humility. The story is told of a Mennonite family riding home from meeting at Franconia, Pennsylvania. The father remarked to his wife with some satisfaction, "I believe we were about the plainest that were there this morning."

The Coat

Once my grandmother gave me a coat.
A suit coat.
It was black, but it was a good coat.
She said it was my grandfather's when he was
   young.
I was about fourteen.
I put it on, and I thought,
"Hey, this is a good coat.
There's some good use left in this coat.
I know it looks sort of out of date.
Actually, it looks sort of strange.
No shoulder-pads.
But why not wear it?
Around home, anyway.
And just to think, it was Grampop's.
Maybe he wore it the first night he came to see
   Grammy.
There's something good about keeping the
   generations connected, that way."

Then after awhile I felt it pricking my neck.
It was horse-hairs, coming through the collar.
I thought, "My, they used to put up with a lot."
It got more and more irritating.
So, though it made me feel a little sad to do it,
I threw the coat away.
Probably Riemer, the rag-man, got it.
That way somebody would get some use out of it.

But you sort of hate to be the one who gives up on
   something
That survived until your generation.
The thing is, after you throw it away,
Nobody else can choose to keep it.
                                        —*John L. Ruth*

"Simple, Substantial and Beautiful"

Most of the Mennonites who came to Pennsylvania soon after its founding had not been allowed by their former European governments to have special houses of worship. They were accustomed to meeting in houses, barns and even forests or caves. But by 1730, tradition holds, they erected a meetinghouse just west of the new town of Lancaster, and from then on such buildings — often doubling as schoolhouses — became common.

In appearance they resembled enlarged houses with extra windows, and a large main room. They were not "sanctuaries," and they contained no altars or pulpits (except in the settlement closer to Philadelphia). In fact, many of the Lancaster County congregations continued for decades to meet in farmhouses, with the preachers and best male singers sitting around the family table. When meetinghouses were finally built, this format was brought along. Eventually "the singers' table" became the feature that corresponded to the pulpit, which was adopted by the more progressive Mennonites.

Those Amish who are more strict do not have even this much church furniture. They use rows of benches in several adjoining rooms of a farmhouse (or barn, shop, etc.).

The early American rural church buildings of Baptists, Presbyterians, Reformed and Methodists were, externally, hardly fancier than those of the Mennonites. But when affluence made them pos-

sible, steeples and Gothic flourishes changed the meetinghouses into churches. Lacking appreciation for these features, Mennonites viewed them under the rubric of pride. To dominate the landscape with a towering spire tipped with the cross that had originally symbolized rejection did not seem consistent with the Christ who had borne it.

The plain people's worship service was as simple and non-liturgical as their architecture. The light that fell across their closely gathered, plain-clad bodies, crowned, on the women's side, with a sea of white, ribboned caps, had passed through no hued glass. The earnest, unison singing was unembroidered by instruments. A tone of lament edged the ministers' chanted discourses — evoking the sadness felt through centuries of persecution. Without even distinguishing the words, the children heard in this tone both history and theology.

The gathering was, and is, less an audience than an enlarged family in a session of family worship. But without the more usual visual symbols, how do these people focus their consciousness?

If for the Catholic the experience culminates in the "This is my Body"; if for the "charismatic" Christian worship crests in an ecstatic release from the limits of words; or if for a "main-line Protestant" a well-crafted sermon may capture the experience of faith — then we might ask how the undemonstrative plain people symbolize theirs.

For them, eternity breaks into time with the sensation of community — the spiritual family. This is more than the promise of salvation; it is already, in time, a part of the experience of it.

What touches the soul to the quick is not a willed or trendy togetherness, but a fellowship grounded solemnly in the memory of the sacrifical gift Christ made of himself. And it is crucial for "Anabaptists" not merely to contemplate and marvel at his sacrifice; they believe we must participate in it by likewise giving ourselves, in the decisive relinquishment of personal autonomy Christ called for and modeled.

To sit in a roomful of people with whom you share this relinquishment, this *Gelassenheit,* this initiation into the defeat of the Cross which is God's victory, this yielding up of even the "natural" right of self-preservation, this fellowship rejected in principle by the wise and powerful of "this world"; to sense the blending of your thoughts and prayers and voice with those of others who would give their lives for you; to think of God in the presence of the brother who has vigorously called you to account, and the family that will surround you physically as well as ideally, as a matter of course, should you experience disaster — this is to feel (alas, sometimes to take for granted) a powerful deliverance.

The barn-raising is, after all, as much the symbol of the plain people's faith as is the steeple the symbol of their neighbors'.

A house in which babies are born, weddings are celebrated, and in which grandparents die, tends to bulge, to grow organically. The emerging design expresses the life of a trans-generational family: here a porch, there a retired parents' addition, there an extra kitchen for newlyweds. Of such a well-kept house an old Mennonite minister once remarked, "Here it looks as though somebody is at home."

"The buildings of these old villages are plain and substantial, but have about them the evidence of the solid comforts and necessities of life characteristic of the unassuming and self-denying people who possess and inhabit them."

—*Descriptions of a Mennonite Community, circa 1886*

"Our new meetinghouse should be simple, substantial, and beautiful."

—Mennonite minister,
Lancaster County

"There is no intention to erect a splendid temple, according to ornament and pride. No superfluities or unnecessaries are intended; rather, only what is serviceable, orderly, becoming, and enduring."

—Henry Clemens,
Mennonite deacon, 1841

To go to "meeting" rather than to "church" was the phrasing of more than Mennonites, Amish, Brethren, and Quakers. It was appropriate for Christians in the dissenting communions of England as well.

The church is the "circle," the gathering of people, no matter what kind of "house" they meet in. The ground we stand on is holy, not because we have erected a shrine, decorated it, filled it with incense, and "dedicated" it, but because God meets us there.

"We believe that the Lord has blessed us with our children and that it is our duty to teach them the ways of honesty, integrity, simple living, and the fear of God."

—Court testimony of Old Order Mennonites of Ontario at a hearing regarding compulsory high school education

"The country? Rural America? That is a joke. . . . Rural America doesn't even exist anymore, not even the farms. . . ."

—a mayor of New York City

"America's greatest asset today is farmland and the people who will bend low to work it."

—Amish minister, 1977

"I don't see beauty in expensive goods. I see beauty in woodwork. Woodworking to me is building barns and putting up anything in the oldfashioned way. . . .

"Why, I see beauty in these old timbers, all these old boards. I see beauty in each part of the barn here. I see beauty in the hay crop here and I even see beauty in the way the bales are stacked. . . .

"I still regret some of the beauties you don't see anymore, like the sheaves of wheat and the straw stacked in front of the barn. . . .

"Every hour of the day, there's beauty to think about being close to nature on the family farm."

—Old Order Mennonite farmer

"Beauty is its own ornament."

Paradoxically, the plain people have room, within their scrupulosity, to abound as well as to be abased. Whatever is permitted is done well.

"You should have some craft in what you make."
— *Advice of an old Mennonite preacher to his grandson*

"Don't get bigger; get better."
— *Retired Mennonite farmer*

"The Hutterite faience differs from the products of other countries in the choice of motif used in decoration. Pictures and figures that might be offensive to religious sensibilities they avoided. By principle they never pictured the human figure. Even animal figures are absent. Plant forms were the favorite motifs. The shapes were also limited. . . .

"When the Hutterites were expelled from Moravia in 1622, they took the secret of China manufacture with them. They used not only special kinds of yellow and white clay, some of which they had to get from distant places, but also definite dyes and mixtures for the ornamentation of the glaze. They observed a process of their own in the manufacture, with a constantly growing feeling for good form, for lively but harmoniously shaded colors, which we still admire. It was actually impossible to find an equivalent substitute for their work."

—*Mennonite Encyclopedia*

The quilt begins as a way for frugal housewives to use even leftover scraps of cloth, and ends, almost in spite of its plain makers' sobriety, as an expression of happiness and work of art.

Whatsoever thy hand findeth to do, do it with thy might.

Ecclesiastes 9:10

She looketh well to the ways of her household, and eateth not the bread of idleness.

Proverbs 31:27

Strength and honour are her clothing; and she shall rejoice in time to come.

Proverbs 31:21

56

Fraktur — a tradition of ornamental calligraphy as old as the Middle Ages — had a vigorous folk revival in both Europe and Pennsylvania in the century after 1750. Pennsylvania's plain people found its bright birds, hearts and flowers unthreatening, as their schoolteachers, many of whom were not themselves of "plain" communions, employed *Fraktur* art to reward pupils or to inscribe the flyleaves of new songbooks with the owners' names. One major use of *Fraktur* — in baptismal certificates — was not applicable to the plain families, since they did not baptize their children at birth. Often the brightest of colors and the most ebullient calligraphic flourishes reinforce the teaching of *Demuth* (humility). Nearly a thousand surviving examples of this art have been identified as coming from eastern Pennsylvania Mennonite homes.

Humus and Humanity

"America's greatest asset," wrote an Amish minister in 1977, "is farmland and the people who will bend low to work it." There is a great difference between people who must, and those who are willing to, "bend low."

Land and people are always linked in the plain people's mentality. "As the land, so the people," remarked a Mennonite farmer to his grandson in 1948. The condition of the land reflects the character of the people.

In 1984 an Amishman from limestone-rich Lancaster County was asked how he could keep his spiritual perspective, when he was privileged to live on some of the world's most productive land. The elderly farmer clarified the situation with a little history.

"Around World War II," he recalled, "there were too many of our young men on our farms here north of the Lincoln Highway. In order to place them on farms, our people had to buy land somewhere else, and they found farms that could be bought cheap in Chester County. The people there, it seemed, had just taken what they could out of the soil year after year until there was hardly anything left. It seems they just hung on until they had gotten the last drop out of it. Things just wouldn't grow anymore. Then they sold.

"We up here pitied those of our people who had to go down there, but after about five years, it started to

yield better and better, until today there's very little difference between what our land produces and what they can get."

A visitor to a southwestern Pennsylvania rural community noticed the huge scar of a strip-mine on the side of a hill. Stopping a passing Amish wagon, he asked the driver, a young farmer, whether such disturbed land could ever be farmed again.

"Yes," replied the Amishman, as six small bonneted and straw-hatted heads rose from out of the back of the wagon.

"How long would it take?" queried the stranger.

"You could build it up in about five years."

The Old Order Amishman, in the age of space-travel, still feels the clods breaking under his shoes, and he leans against the slope of the hill instead of riding cushioned in an air-conditioned tractor cab. His farm produces at least as much per acre as the best among his more secular neighbors. True, his life is often too basic to seem like an option for others, who belong to what he tends to call the "higher" churches. What they see as a great day for a trip, he finds a good day for work on the land. But in his humility, the Amishman feels an inarticulate communion with his infinite Maker. He feels that his breath is continuous with what God breathed into the dust of the earth, making man a living soul. The soil is thus not only sacred, but kin.

In an age which offers seminars in "assertiveness" and the art of gaining "a good self-image," the plain people are heading in the opposite direction. A course in humility is not likely to be in the curriculum outside their church. The burden of proof today is always on those calling for humility, and they are suspected of either ulterior motives or poor emotional health. It is all but impossible, in such an atmosphere, to respect the statement made by a Dutch Mennonite writer in 1664: "It behooves and becomes a right and true Christian that he should be little and low in the World, and shun the greatness of the same, and keep himself like the lowly ones." Just as startling are the words written by a Mennonite minister near Lancaster in 1775, in an appeal to the Pennsylvania Assembly: "We think ourselves very weak to give God his due Honor, He being a Spirit and Life, and we only Dust and Ashes."

"Don't run yourself down like that," urges the spirit of our age. "Tell yourself, 'I'm good!' "

But where is the proof of our wisdom? In our broken marriages, our exploited land, our international threatenings? Do they demonstrate a high valuation of life's gifts?

And can we really say that the world-forsaking plain people, clinging to their farmland or traveling to find other ground, do not cherish the earth and keep it?

When they say, "We must obey God rather than man," are they not being faithful citizens of Creation?

Without raising their voices, have they not made a statement?

There is a variously-told story of a plain-dressed Dunkard accosted on the street of a Pennsylvania town by an evangelical young man who asked, "Brother, are you saved?"

The long-bearded Dunkard did not respond verbally immediately. He pulled out a piece of paper and wrote on it, then handed it to the stranger. "Here," he said, "are the names and addresses of my family, neighbors, and people I do business with. Ask them if they think I'm saved. I could tell you anything."

In an eastern Pennsylvania supermarket checkout line, a woman in a long black cape dress and bonnet began writing a check as her groceries were tallied.

"Do you have a check-cashing card for this store?" asked the clerk.

"No, I don't."

"What about a credit card?"

"Sorry, no."

"A driver's license, then! You have to have some identification. What *do* you have?"

"I don't have any of those things. I just have trust."

With a glance at face and garb, the manager initialed her check. The clerk rolled her eyes to the ceiling in mock horror, saying, "Some people have got their nerve!"

—*Doris Janzen Longacre,*
Living More With Less

Ye are the salt of the earth: but if the salt have lost his savour, wherewith shall it be salted? it is thenceforth good for nothing, but to be cast out, and to be trodden under foot of men.

Ye are the light of the world. A city that is set on an hill cannot be hid.

Neither do men light a candle, and put it under a bushel, but on a candlestick; and it giveth light unto all that are in the house.

Let your light so shine before men, that they may see your good works, and glorify your Father which is in heaven.

Matthew 5:13-16

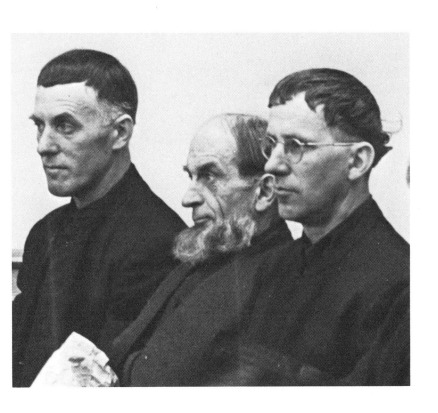

"When we give bread to the hungry, shelter to the homeless, and clothing and bedding to those who are cold, light and health enter our house and our life. Then there is nothing we need in the whole world, for our thoughts are filled with God and His Kingdom. It is not in the fasting or the sacrifice itself that we meet God. In fasting as in sacrifice, it is not the cult or the solemn ceremony that moves Him. He does not want them. What he does want and demand is what is good: justice, love, and good deeds. There is a thirst for the living God at work in all these things, pointing to the salvation and healing which is in Jesus Christ. Then the heavens are opened. Then comes the One who was to come."

—*Andreas Ehrenpreis, 1650*

Blessed Are the Peacemakers

The Germanic plain people of today stem from those elements of the diverse Anabaptist movements that reacted away from attempts at violent revolution or reform. In 1527 some Anabaptists in South Germany and Switzerland agreed that the use of force, though divinely sanctioned for governmental keeping of order in a diverse human society, is not to be a part of the society that takes Christ's order as its own — the Church. A decade later other Anabaptists in the Netherlands, having observed the dismaying results of a violent Anabaptist takeover of the city of Muenster, were gathered by Menno Simons into a simple fellowship that tried, in the name of Christ and his cross, to separate itself from all violence.

From these beginnings there has come a continuous Christian fellowship in which, for four and a half centuries, rejection of "the sword" has been essential for membership. It remains so for all who are still plain people, though some of their "progressive" cousins have embarrassed them by keeping the name Mennonite or Brethren while changing their views on this point. For those who have maintained the plain life, non-violence (or "non-resistance," as they prefer to call it) is not a mere ornament to the teachings of Christ, nor just an ideal to be praised, nor simply a fulfillment to be anticipated in a future dispensation, nor a heritage to be only remembered. It is an essential element in what Christ taught and did himself. The plain people do

not have a theology which detaches Christ's sacrificial atonement for the sin of the world from his showing, thereby, a better way — the only right way — for human beings to live.

They believe it is more important for us to bear witness to the reality of God's love than it is to preserve our own lives, which are in God's keeping. "You have heard it said that you should love your neighbor and hate your enemy. But I say to you, love your enemies . . . so that you may be the children of your Father in heaven, who makes his sun to rise on the evil and the good . . ."

Note well, however, that this is not the same as saying, "Love your enemies so that you will deserve God's forgiveness." Plain people, who are seldom highly articulate in explaining their implicit theology, have often been accused by "evangelical" Christians of believing that they earn their salvation by what they *do*. Rather, they believe that they must love their enemies *because* God has forgiven them. And from another side, they love their enemies, *because* the Kingdom of God is, in Christ's words, already "at hand."

From time to time Mennonites and Brethren are "discovered" by "peace people" who see in these groups potential for a new pacifist movement. But a disappointment often occurs, when it inevitably becomes clear that the plain people base their pacifism (a word with which they are uncomfortable for its possibly humanist associations) on obedience to Christ rather than on a hope that humanity might be persuaded to come to its senses.

It is more important to these folk that children grow up in a stable family environment than that their parents travel to march or speak. When Three Mile Island threatened a nuclear catastrophe, they hardly raised an eyebrow in their nearby communities, feeling that God, rather than humans, was in control here. Thus they managed, in their "nonresistant" beliefs, to offend both evangelicals and liberal activists. Their failure to trouble themselves about the world's suicidal madness is, indeed, not always spiritually impressive. While conflagration looms, they can be debating whether or not to have inflated rubber tires. They tend to work on only some of the issues on the moral spectrum.

But in refusing to lend a hand to the machinery of war through the centuries, and by continuing to teach emphatically this heritage to the present generation, the plain people have made a point: it is possible for human beings not to murder each other. That is their testimony, and as much of a protest as we shall hear from them. For them, the war has been over for two millennia. As one of their very first leaders, Conrad Grebel of Zurich, wrote in 1524, the new order of Christ "and its adherents are not to be protected by the sword . . . nor do they use worldly sword or war, since all killing has ceased with them." That fact, to the plain people, is bedrock reality.

". . . Since Christians must not . . . practice vengeance, neither can they make the weapons by which . . . vengeance and destruction may be practiced by others . . . . Therefore we make neither swords, spears, guns nor any such weapons. However, whatever is made for the benefit and daily use of man, such as bread-knives, axes, hoes, and the like, we can and do make."

—Peter Rideman, 1541

"We German Baptists (called Tunkers) do most solemnly believe that the bearing of carnal weapons in order to destroy life, is in direct opposition to the Gospel of Christ, which we accept as the rule of our faith and practice. To this we have most solemnly vowed to be true until death."

—John Kline, 1861

Reflections at Verdun, 1952

I stood in the Ossuary in France —
    The Hall of dead men's bones;
I walked by the large sarcophagi,
    On the marble, memorial stones.

Down in the crypt beneath the Hall,
    In bins stacked side by side,
Are heaps of bones from the battlefield,
    Where carnage had scattered them wide.

All intellect gone from the empty skulls!
    Destroyed, every medium of skill!
Sturdy young forms that had housed men's souls
    Lie broken and mingled and still.

That summer morn as I stood in France
    And gazed on those stacks of bones,
My outer ear listened to songs of birds;
    My inner ear listened to moans.

It seemed a soft, pattering sound I sensed,
    Not of raindrops, but of tears
Still shed by mothers, sweethearts, and wives,
    Grieving through passing years:

Mothers mourning for stalwart sons
    Cut down by the god of War;
Wives for husbands who said good-by,
    And returned to them never more.

The tears of sweethearts, too, I heard,
    Dropping that summer morn,
Weeping for dream-homes ever unbuilt,
    Children forever unborn.

Would God that despots and makers of war,
    With fame and prestige as their goals,
Would gaze at that crypt and count the cost —
    The price in bodies and souls.

—*Myra K. Lehman*

"It is our fixed Principle, rather than take up Arms to defend our King, our Country, or our Selves, to suffer all that is dear to us to be rent from us, even Life itself, and this we think not out of Contempt to Authority, but that herein we act agreeable to what we think is the Mind and Will of our Lord Jesus."

—*Thirteen Mennonite Ministers, 1755*

"We have dedicated ourselves to serve all Men in every Thing that can be helpful to the Preservation of Men's Lives, but we find no Freedom in giving, or doing, or assisting in any Thing by which Men's Lives are destroyed or hurt. We beg the Patience of all those who believe we err in this Point."

—*Benjamin Hershey, 1775*

Salt and Light

The most conservative of the plain people are often slow, even reluctant, to make verbal declarations of their faith in settings outside their meetings, schools and homes.

Most Mennonites and Brethren find this inconsistent not only with their own spiritual origins, but with the biblical model of the Christian church as well. Whereas Jesus prayed that his disciples would be "in the world but not of the world," we can be so socially separate that we are not even "in the world."

Yet there are elements in the Old Order witness that have a paradoxical logic. Try to explain to an Amish family that their life has no message as millions of curious tourists from cities around the world cruise annually by their front porch. It isn't only the advertisements by the Tourist Bureau that bring this influx.

One of the deepest instincts in those who inherit Anabaptist teaching is for practicality. What is ortho-doxy without ortho-praxis? The way spiritual ideas *work* in individual, family and community behavior is the test of their truth. Instead of considering the Apostle James's admonitions as "right strawy" — as Martin Luther did — the Anabaptists rejoiced in James's spelling out of how behavior should reflect what he called "the royal" or "perfect law" of love and liberty. After all, if faith is the evidence of things not seen, what is the evidence of faith? Is it in what we say, or what we do? Is it in

whether or not we are praying at the altar, or in whether or not we have "first" (as Jesus put it) gone to be reconciled with our brother?

The plain people at least offer a visual profile of their faith-community. If you want to find an Amishman, you will be able to see him. Can as much be said for the Christianity of a person whose faith is all "in his heart," but who pays no social price whatever for "having" it?

A truly Christian community not only has a message — it *is* one, in the very shape it takes and the possibilities it demonstrates. It is also a message in the seasoning effect (or lack of it) that it works on its surrounding society. If it can't be "tasted," is it there?

It is one thing to argue for pacifism, and quite another to refuse to sue for one's rights even if one has legal justification for doing so. The plain people do not allow their members to sue, and expel from the church any who do. They quote the Apostle's question, "Why do you not rather take wrong?"

To ask for the privilege of "affirming" rather than

swearing, when called into court, is not only to acknowledge the authority of Christ's specific teaching. It is also confessing that one does not recognize special circumstances under which one *really* tells the truth, as opposed to ordinary times when there is no penalty for lying. Persons whose word is as good as their bond do less to subsidize lawyers, and add strength to the community.

A returned soldier who had lost an arm in a foreign campaign during World War II expressed his feelings during the national Bicentennial in 1976. Speaking to his Mennonite neighbors in southeastern Pennsylvania, he said, "I don't agree with your pacifism, but I appreciate the fact that after I had gone away to fight, there was a community at home with a quality that was worth coming back to."

When the most conservative of the plain people go with the Mennonite Disaster Service to help clean up after a flood or hurricane, they have no publicity committee. In fact, they have been known to refuse to leave the bus if there were photographers present from the media. High-ranking officials from the state government have been entertained, in groups, on Amish farms, but only on the condition that the media would not be present, nor the story circulated. If they are praised in the papers for good deeds, these people fear they may be in the category of those Jesus described as making a show of their virtue; once they have been noticed, he said, "They have their reward."

Our culture pays attention to the exciting, the dramatic, and the radical. But if "to excite" means to cause to happen, if "drama" is the "doing" of something, and "radical" going to the "root" of the situation, what better fulfills these meanings than maintaining a loving, stable community? What is more humane than obeying this divine command?

". . . Humility and humanity are closely related. The old Latin grammarians believed that the words *humilitas* and *humanitas* were both derived from *humus*, the earth. . . . God. . .is called the Most High but he has been pleased to make himself known as the Most Low."

—*John Macquarrie,*
The Humility of God

. . . A man's life consisteth not in the abundance of the things which he possesseth.

Luke 12:15

. . . The meek shall inherit the earth; and shall delight themselves in the abundance of peace.

Psalm 37:11

"I always liked land."

—*Old Order Mennonite preacher,*
Ontario

Ye call me Master and Lord: and ye say well; for so I am.

If I then, your Lord and Master, have washed your feet; ye also ought to wash one another's feet.

For I have given you an example, that ye should do as I have done to you.

If ye know these things, happy are ye if ye do them.

John 13:13-15, 17

It would not agree with the principles of the gospel, such as humility, non-conformity to the world, etc., to erect large and expensive tombstones.

He hath shewed thee, O man, what is good; and what doth the Lord require of thee, but to do justly, and to love mercy, and to walk humbly with thy God?

Micah 6:8

Notes on Photographs

(In deference to the style of this book, captions do not appear with each photo; however, because some of the photos include unusual scenes and information which may elude the average reader, the following notes may prove helpful. Numbers correspond to the pages on which the photos appear.)

7. An Amish man from Shipshewana, Indiana, wearing broadfall pants and suspenders without buckles. The characteristic Indiana-style buggy can be seen in the background.

8. Old Colony Mennonite schoolgirls in Mexico. These German-speaking people moved from Russia to Manitoba, Canada, in the 1870s and thence to Mexico in the 1920s.

11. A Hutterite family in South Dakota studies the Bible. This branch of the Anabaptist family practices communal living.

14. Old Order Mennonites on a back road in Waterloo County, Ontario.

19. A member of the ultra-conservative Swartzentruber Amish in Ohio converses with a friend.

22. Two Hutterite girls prepare *Zweibach* buns to be baked.

25. A Mennonite quilter of the Morgantown, Pennsylvania, area.

26. A group at the annual meeting of the Old German Baptist Brethren Church (Old Order Dunkers).

31. An unidentified Lancaster, Pennsylvania, Mennonite couple of the early 1900s.

40. The Mohler Church of the Brethren, near Ephrata, Pennsylvania, ca. 1915.

43. The interior of the Mohler Church of the Brethren, ca. 1915.

46. Wheat shocks form a geometric pattern in Lancaster County, Pennsylvania.

51. An Old Colony Mennonite woman in Mexico operates her treadle sewing machine.

63. An Old German Baptist Brethren patriarch.

64. A "Swiss" Amish couple inspect merchandise in Berne, Indiana.

67. Two Old Order Mennonites and an Old Order Amish man appear in an Ontario courtroom.

68. (top) Conservative Mennonite volunteers help with a Mennonite Disaster service (MDS) project in Alabama. MDS aids victims of natural tragedies in a way similar to the Red Cross.

68. (bottom) An Old Order Amish man operates a hand cultivator.

71. An amused Amish man in his buggy at Shipshewana, Indiana.

76. An Amish girl from Berne, Indiana, enjoying the flowers.

82. An Amish group from Buchanan County, Iowa, enjoying an outing.

89. Towels and basin as used in the practice of feetwashing — symbolic of Christ's humility — in many plain churches.

92. Old Order Mennonite vehicles in Waterloo County, Ontario.

Readings and Sources

Bender, H.S. *The Anabaptist Vision.* Scottdale, Pennsylvania: Herald Press, 1955. Classic recent statement; a scholarly pamphlet.

Braght, Thieleman J. van. *The Bloody Theater, or Martyrs Mirror.* Scottdale, Pennsylvania: Herald Press, 1950. Seventeenth-century saga of suffering of Mennonites at the inception of their fellowship. 1500 large pages.

Burkholder, J. R. and Calvin Redekop, ed. *Kingdom, Cross and Community.* Scottdale, Pennsylvania: Herald Press, 1976. Scholarly self-assessment by Mennonites in cultural transition.

Denlinger, A. Martha. *Real People.* Scottdale, Pennsylvania: Herald Press, 1975. Observations on the life of the plain people by one who has lived that way herself.

Dyck, Cornelius J., ed. *An Introduction to Mennonite History.* Scottdale, Pennsylvania: Herald Press, 1967, 1981. The best short introduction available.

Epp, Frank H. *Mennonites in Canada 1786-1820: The History of a Separate People.* New York: MacMillan, 1974. The best-written volume of North American Mennonite history.

Estep, William. *The Anabaptist Story.* Grand Rapids: Eerdmans, 1975. Backgrounds of today's Mennonites, Amish and Baptists, in a readable, accurate narrative.

Fisher, Gideon L. *Farm Life and Its Changes.* Gordonville, Pennsylvania: Pequea Publishers, 1978. An unusual book, written by an Amishman; authentic Amish viewpoint.

Gingerich, Melvin. *Mennonite Attire Through the Centuries.* Breinigsville, Pennsylvania: Pennsylvania German Society, 1970. A survey of the "plain clothes" phenomenon, with many authentic photos.

Good, Merle. *Hazel's People.* Scottdale, Pennsylvania: Herald Press, 1971. A novel set among the Mennonite community of Lancaster County, Pennsylvania, written by a Mennonite.

_____ . *These People Mine.* Scottdale, Pennsylvania: Herald Press, 1973. A poetic evocation of the thread of Mennonite identity and peoplehood.

Horst, Mary Ann. *My Old Order Mennonite Heritage.* Kitchener, Ontario: Pennsylvania Dutch Craft Shop, 1972. A book of respectful, authentic, non-sophisticated observations.

Hostetler, John A. *Amish Life.* Scottdale, Pennsylvania: Herald Press, 1959. A popular and authentic booklet on the topic.

_____ . *Amish Society.* Baltimore: Johns Hopkins University Press, 1968. The best scholarly treatment.

_____ . *Hutterite Life.* Scottdale, Pennsylvania: Herald Press, 1965. Popular and authentic booklet.

_____ . *Hutterite Society.* Baltimore: Johns Hopkins University Press, 1974. Widely praised scholarly study.

_____ . *Mennonite Life.* Scottdale, Pennsylvania: Herald Press, 1959. Popular and authentic booklet.

Keim, Albert N. *Compulsory Education and the Amish: The Right Not to Be Modern.* Boston: Beacon Press, 1975. A source book which tells an engaging story of steadfast resistance to secularism.

Klaassen, Walter. *Anabaptism in Outline: Selected Primary Sources*. Scottdale, Pennsylvania: Herald Press, 1981. A unique anthology of original Anabaptist writings in fresh translations.

—————. *Anabaptism: Neither Catholic Nor Protestant*. Waterloo, Ontario: Conrad Press, 1972. Excellent discussion of the core values and teachings of the spiritual movement behind the modern-day "plain people."

Kraybill, Donald B. *The Upside-Down Kingdom*. Scottdale, Pennsylvania: Herald Press, 1978. A Lancaster County sociology professor spells out the practical applications of the New Testament.

Longacre, Doris Janzen. *More-with-Less Cookbook*. Scottdale, Pennsylvania: Herald Press, 1976. A unique cookbook drawing on the tradition of stewardship and frugality in Mennonite heritage, without neglecting the motif of enjoyment of good food.

Martin, Earl S. *Reaching the Other Side*. New York: Crown Publishers, 1978. A Mennonite couple in Vietnam — but for aid instead of war.

Mennonite Encyclopedia, The. Scottdale, Pennsylvania: Herald Press, 1959. Four large volumes on practically everything Mennonite-related.

Mennonite World Handbook. Lombard, Illinois: Mennonite World Conference, 1978. A mini-encyclopedia.

Miller, John W. *The Christian Way*. Scottdale, Pennsylvania: Herald Press, 1969. A reflection on the Sermon on the Mount by a Mennonite teacher.

Ruth, John L. *Maintaining the Right Fellowship*. Scottdale, Pennsylvania: Herald Press, 1984. A narrative account of life in the oldest Mennonite community in America.

—————. *Mennonite Identity and Literary Art*. Scottdale, Pennsylvania: Herald Press, 1978. Four lectures aimed at Mennonite writers.

—————. *The Amish: A People of Preservation*. Distributed by Encyclopedia Britannica Films. A 1-hour documentary which appeared on the PBS Network.

—————. *The Hutterites: To Care and Not to Care*. With Burton Buller and John A. Hostetler, distributed by Buller Films, Inc., Henderson, Nebraska. A 1-hour documentary which appeared on the PBS Network.

—————. *'Twas Seeding Time*. Scottdale, Pennsylvania: Herald Press, 1976. How Mennonites experienced the American Revolution.

Showalter, Mary Emma. *Mennonite Community Cookbook*. Scottdale, Pennsylvania: Herald Press, 1957. The best of the "plenty" tradition.

Sider, Ronald J. *Rich Christians in an Age of Hunger*. Downers Grove, Illinois: Inter-Varsity Press, 1977, 1984. A Brethren in Christ teacher writes of simplicity, compassion, stewardship and obedience.

Wenger, J. C. *Mennonite Faith Series*. Scottdale, Pennsylvania: Herald Press, 1977. A series of popular pamphlets on Mennonite faith, life and origins.

Yoder, John H. *The Politics of Jesus*. Grand Rapids: Eerdmans, 1972. A widely read and quoted study, expressing the core insights of Anabaptist teachings in contemporary terms.

The Author

John L. Ruth is known and loved as a storyteller and historian. Captured by the spirit and past of his people, he has spent recent years interpreting, writing about, and filming the tradition and faith of Mennonite, Amish and Hutterite groups.

Ruth grew up in the Franconia area of eastern Pennsylvania, where he lives today. An ordained Mennonite minister, he spent much of his life in the world of English, graduating from Eastern Baptist College (now Eastern College), St. Davids, Pennsylvania, and completing doctoral work in English and American literature at Harvard University in 1968. For 12 years he taught literature at Eastern College and the University of Hamburg, Germany.

He has been involved with the production of films on the Amish (*The Amish: A People of Preservation*) and Hutterites, Mennonites of Ontario and Virginia, pioneer schoolteacher Christopher Dock (*The Quiet in the Land*), and the city of Strasbourg, France (*Strasbourg: City of Hope*). His books include biography (*Conrad Grebel, Son of Zurich*), history ('*Twas Seeding Time: A Mennonite View of the American Revolution; Maintaining the Right Fellowship: A Narrative Account of Life in the Oldest Mennonite Community in America;* a forthcoming history of the Lancaster Mennonite Conference) and four lectures entitled *Mennonite Identity and Literary Art*. He has also written the texts for two musical works, *Christopher Dock* and *Martyrs Mirror*.

He and Roma (Jacobs) are the parents of three grown children.